Mission San Fernando

CALIFORNIA MISSION DAYS *by Helen Bauer*

CALIFORNIA STATE SERIES

Published by
CALIFORNIA STATE DEPARTMENT OF EDUCATION
Sacramento, 1957

ACKNOWLEDGMENTS

THE AUTHOR wishes to acknowledge with gratitude the assistance given by the following persons in the Los Angeles City School system: to Dr. Raymond E. Pollich, Associate Superintendent, Division of Elementary Education, for his reading of the manuscript and for the helpful criticisms given; to Miss Edna Wiese, Middle Academic Supervisor, Valley Elementary District, for her generous help in reading the manuscript and to Marion Horton, Elizabeth Williams, Jasmine Britton, Ann Molloy and my associates in the Curriculum Division for their encouragement and interest. Special acknowledgment is given to Albert J. Dunkel, Audio-Visual Education Section, for his painstaking work in making the drawings and map.

For the pictures of present day missions, credit and appreciation is given to Hubert A. Lowman. To Arthur Barr goes credit for the pictures of mission life. Other sources of picture material to which credit is due and hereby acknowledged are: California Mission Trails, California Historical Society and the Society of California Pioneers.

To the editorial staff of the publisher for valuable editorial assistance.

Acknowledgment is made to my husband, always patient and understanding. Last and most of all to my son, Sherwin Carlquist, without whose urging, deserved criticisms and constant faith, this book would never have been written.

printed in
CALIFORNIA STATE PRINTING OFFICE
SACRAMENTO 2ND PRINT, 30M 1958

FOREWORD

THE MISSIONS were very important to the early life of California. They were the first step in the colonization of California after the explorers had found it. The purpose of the missions was to Christianize the Indians, raise their standard of living, and to protect Spain's claim for holding this new land.

The fascinating history of California is a heritage that belongs to every boy and girl in the state. With this in mind, the author has emphasized the qualities of courage and heroism of the padres of the early missions. The text is not only interesting but it presents an intriguing story of each mission, bringing out details which made each mission individually famous. Here is a book that links the past with the present in such a way that those who read the stories will be interested in the happenings of those bygone days as they affected the lives of men, women, and children who lived then. In a simple way it brings life and action from the past so that the happenings portrayed there are so real, so adventurous, so thrilling, that no fiction need embellish it.

Not the least important part of the book is the authentic pictures of each mission showing them as they were when the padres left them and as they now may be seen. There is no other book in print today that shows these old missions, and so this will meet a long-felt need. Many misconceptions of early mission life have been built up in the minds of children by the use of only modern mission pictures.

Thus, through pictures as well as text, the historical past is linked with the present. General readers will also find this book a ready source of authentic and up-to-date pictorial material.

The author has made an honest endeavor to meet a real need in our California schools in those grades studying California history. It is an attempt to present the history of the missions in so simple and interesting a way that children may read it with pleasure. It is hoped that it will provide a welcome source of material for teachers who need more available material for this period of California history. If those who read about the missions find enjoyment, interest, a desire to visit the missions, and a respect for the background of our state, this book will have made its contribution.

Dr. Raymond E. Pollich
ASSOCIATE SUPERINTENDENT, ELEMENTARY ED. DIV.
LOS ANGELES CITY SCHOOLS

PREFACE

THERE IS ALWAYS something exciting and interesting in the story of the early days in California. This book tells the stories of the padres who walked up and down the state of California and founded twenty-one missions. The road they walked from San Diego in the south to Sonoma in the north was called El Camino Real, or the Royal Highway. This road probably had more history and adventure connected with it than any other road in the New World.

While there was much about the missions that was the same, there were many things that made each mission different from the rest. Each mission had its own story of adventure to tell, and you will want to find out what made each one famous. You will want to read about the missions for their history. You will want to know of the good their builders did. You will want to know what the padres did for the Indians and how the Indians lived and helped in the building of the missions.

These stories are told to you in the order in which the padres founded the missions. With each story there is a picture which shows how the mission looked when the padres left it. Perhaps you can imagine just how the padres and the Indians worked and lived at that time. There are pictures of the missions showing how they look today.

All of the twenty-one missions are still left in California for you to see. It is the hope of the author that all who read these stories will want to visit many of the missions. As you stand inside their old adobe walls, think of the days of the padres and of the work that was done there. From these visits you will gain added interest and you will learn how important the missions were to the early life of California.

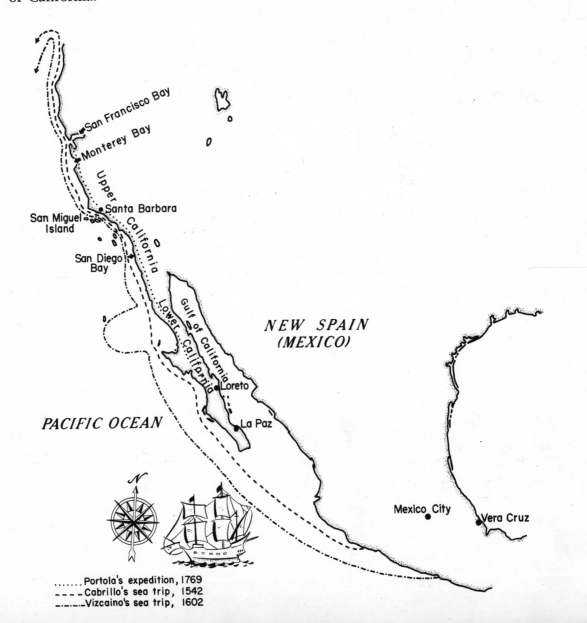

.... Portola's expedition, 1769
- - - - Cabrillo's sea trip, 1542
-...-...- Vizcaino's sea trip, 1602

CONTENTS

BEFORE THE DAYS OF THE MISSIONS *Spanish explorers seek a California harbor*

THE STORY of California's missions began a long time ago. It really began two hundred years before the first mission was started. The story began in the far countries of the world that knew about America. Spain first sent ships to explore this new land. For a long time all the land in America belonged to Spain.

Spanish people who came to America lived in the part we call Mexico. They called it New Spain. These people were looking for silver and gold. Rich mines were found, but always they wanted more. Indians told the Spanish of more gold in the west. On they pushed to find it!

On the west coast of Mexico little towns were built. Now it was easy to send ships out onto the Pacific Ocean. Ships went to China and India for silks and spices. The sailors wanted to get back quickly with their rich cargo. Something kept them from doing this. Strong winds that blew them westward from Mexico through the South Pacific kept them from coming back the same way. When the ships went north, the winds blew them back to America. Still they were a long way from Mexico. There were never enough water and food to last. Many sailors died on the way. A harbor had to be found where ships could stop. A good place for one would be on the coast of California. Then they could stop before going south to Mexico. This would make the long trip much easier.

At this time there was a governor in New Spain called a Viceroy. Viceroy

12

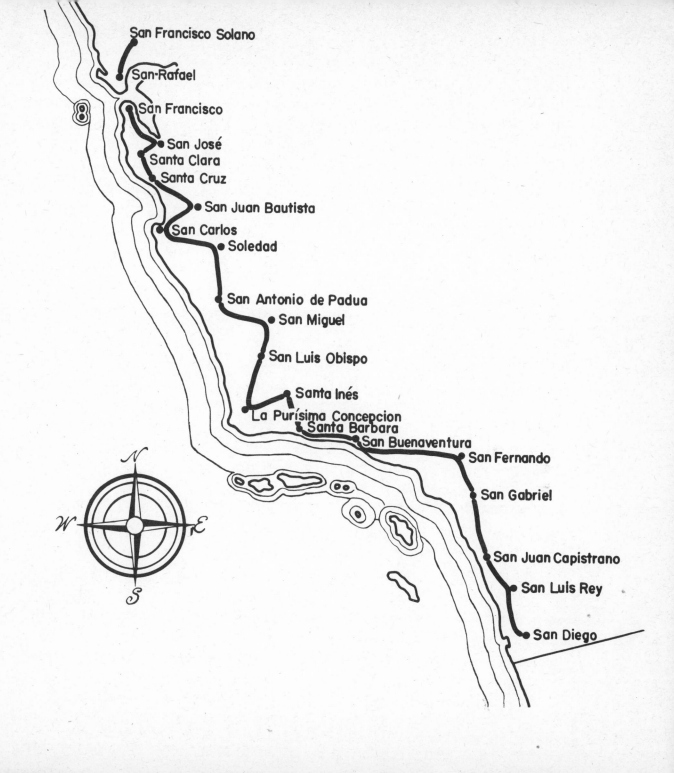

means "in place of the King," and he had been sent by the King of Spain. He was sent to find new harbors on the coast. Then the trip from India would be shorter. North of New Spain was a land that should be explored. The Viceroy chose a good sailor to explore for him. His name was Juan Rodriguez Cabrillo. The Viceroy told him, "Go as far north as you can. Find a place for our ships to land."

Cabrillo and his men left Mexico in two small ships. After three months they came to a bay. Today we call it San Diego Bay. Little did Cabrillo know how important San Diego would become. Here the first California mission would be founded two hundred years later. "This is a good and safe harbor," Cabrillo told his men. "There must be other harbors along the coast." Farther up the coast, Cabrillo saw little plumes of smoke from Indian fires. This was the next stop, which he called Bay of Smokes. The ships sailed north again. They kept close to shore all the way. Near present-day Ventura, Indian canoes darted out into the waves. Cabrillo thought "Canoe Town" would be a good name for this place.

Cabrillo's ships sailed near the Santa Barbara coast. His ships tossed in the waves. They had to seek shelter on a nearby island. Here Cabrillo fell and broke his arm. Even then he had no thought of going back. Storms made the waves rough. No land was in sight. Then Cabrillo saw a curve of land like a bay. It was so stormy that the pine trees could hardly be seen on the shore. It looked like a good harbor, but how could one find out in this weather? Cabrillo was ill and his men were ready for a rest. They turned back at last to the island near Santa Barbara. It was on this island of San Miguel that the sailors buried brave Cabrillo. Now they had to decide where to go. The pilot spoke up, "Let us try again. I promised Cabrillo I would go north once more. The storms will soon be over. Then we can find a harbor." The sailors agreed. They sailed even farther north. Again storms began to beat the little ships. It was too hard to go on. They had sailed past two harbors and did not know it!

14

The Spanish people were excited over news of the voyage. They were glad that a new harbor had been found. The more stories the explorers told, the more the people wanted to hear. "This new land is not like the old California," they said. "It is a rich and beautiful land." After a few years the Spanish people called this long finger of land in Mexico Lower California. This was a dry, rocky land. The beautiful land they had found in the north was Alta or Upper California.

It was a long time before anyone thought about California again. The next Spanish explorer to be sent north was Sebastián Vizcaíno. He was sent by Monterey, a new Viceroy in Mexico. Off he sailed as captain of three small ships. He came to the harbor Cabrillo had found. He gave it the name of San Diego. Farther north he rounded a large curve in the coast. This he called Santa Barbara.

Vizcaíno sailed on north. At last, after many days, he found a large harbor. It was an open bay, shaped like an "O." Along the shore were pine trees. They were tall trees that could be used for masts on ships. Blue lupine and golden poppies were in bloom. Grass was thick and green along the shore. The climate seemed like that of Spain, warm even in December. Vizcaíno named the place Monterey to honor the Viceroy. This was in the year 1602.

Some of the men were tired and sick. One ship took them back to Mexico. The other ship sailed north until storms drove them back. Behind the clouds and fog was the greatest harbor of them all. Who would find San Francisco Bay? Then, strange as it seems, California was forgotten again. Viceroy Monterey had gone back to Spain. A new Viceroy showed no interest.

The years went on and on. For more than a hundred and sixty years no Spanish ships sailed into California harbors. Then someone became interested. Russian ships had landed on the north coast of America. They found it to be a good land for hunting. On the islands were otters and seals. The skins of the animals made good coats. People of cold lands were glad to pay high prices for furs. Now the

Russians were coming nearer and nearer to California. Spain decided to hold this new land.

Now things began to happen quickly! The Viceroy of Mexico said the Russians must be kept out of California. Other countries must not settle there. The King sent an officer, José de Galvez, to help the Viceroy. Galvez went to see the governor of Lower California. He was Gaspar de Portolá, who lived at Loreto. Portolá was much interested. He promised not only to help but also to go along. Someone should go who could teach the Indians in California. Father Junípero Serra was president of the Lower California missions. He knew how to teach. He understood the Indians. He would be just the right person to send. Galvez sent for him to talk over plans.

Father Junípero Serra was delighted. He was more excited than Galvez! He was even more excited than Portolá! This was because Father Serra had a secret. For forty years he had held a dream in his heart. It was a dream of going to California. Now, it seemed to him, at last his dream was coming true.

HOW THE MISSIONS BEGAN
A boy's dream and how it came true

THE MISSIONS of California really began in the dream of a boy. The boy's name was José Serra. He lived on a little island called Majorca, near the coast of Spain.

On the island was a convent. A convent is the home of religious men. These men spend their lives preaching, teaching, and helping people. José went to school at the convent. His teachers belonged to the Order of St. Francis. They wore rough gray robes and slept on narrow beds. They were called Franciscan friars. Friar means "brother."

The friars spoke sometimes of a faraway country called California. In this land lived dark-skinned Indians. They had nobody to teach or to help them. This José longed to do. He dreamed of being a gray-robed friar. He dreamed of crossing the sea in a big ship. He dreamed of going, with gifts in his hands and love in his heart. He wanted to help the Indians of California.

When José was seventeen, part of the dream came true. José was given a robe. He became a Franciscan friar. He was so happy in this new life that he changed his name from José to Junípero. Junípero was the name given to a friend of St. Francis.

Among the younger boys at the convent Junípero Serra found two good friends. Their names were Juan Crespi and Francisco Palou. He told them of his dream, and they shared his hopes. Often the three boys talked together of going to California. Then came their chance to go to Mexico.

Father Serra always remembered well the day they sailed into the peaceful harbor of Vera Cruz. It was two hundred miles from Mexico City. They walked all the way. His leg was hurt on the trip and healed slowly. He began his work in New Spain, or Mexico. He spent twenty years teaching the Indians and building the missions there.

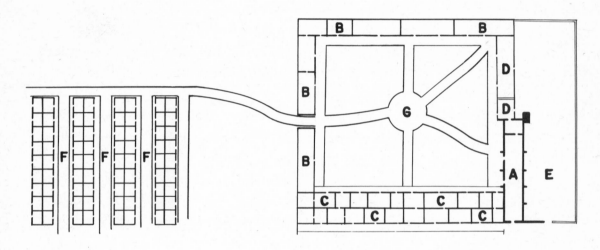

PLAN OF A MISSION

A- Church
B- Workshops
C- Padres' House and
    Guest Rooms

D- Storeroom
E- Cemetery
F- Indian Village
G- Patio

Then Galvez sent for him. "I want you to go Alta California," he said. "I want you to be head of new missions to be built there." They made their plans. At each mission there was to be a church and some workshops. Indians would live in small houses by the mission church. All the buildings would make a small village. Such a village would be called a mission. Padres would teach the Indians to grow crops and raise cattle. They would learn about the Christian religion. Later the missions would become towns, or pueblos. The padres would leave and start other missions. The mission church would become the church in the pueblo. Indians would be given mission land and cattle. After that the Indians could care for themselves.

Father Serra listened carefully. Did he still want to go? This was the chance he had been waiting for, but he was fifty-six years old. Was it too late? It was never too late to help others, he thought. Yes, he wanted to go! He had always wanted to do something like this. Then he thought of his friends, Father Palou and Father Crespi. "May my two friends go with me?" he asked. It was agreed that Father Crespi might go. Father Palou would have to stay.

What exciting days followed! Father Serra collected things they would need from the Lower California missions. He took bright cloth and shiny beads as gifts for the Indians. He took bells that would call them to worship at the missions. Galvez helped get tools, grain, cows, and mules.

"Now, Father Serra," said Galvez, "the first mission must be at San Diego. Later there will be one by Monterey Bay. A mission can then be founded on the coast between the two. We will call it Mission San Buenaventura for good luck."

The expedition was divided into parties. Two parties would go north by ships. Two parties would march north by land. Father Serra wanted to go with the second of the land parties. He put boxes of supplies on board the *San Carlos.* At last everything was ready for the daring adventure!

19

ON TO CALIFORNIA! *Coming of the padres*

THE SAN CARLOS sailed first from La Paz. That was in January, 1769. Before it left, the governor made a long speech. He said, "The King of Spain wants you to do four things. He wants missions to be built in California. He wants you to hold the land for Spain. He wants you to keep out other countries. He wants a town near a harbor where ships may stop to trade. Father Serra will take charge of the new work. Let us hope that all reach the new land safely and have success!"

Wind filled the sails of the *San Carlos* and she was on her way! The *San Antonio,* the other ship, sailed a month later. Soon after this, the first land party started. Father Crespi and Captain Rivera were in this party. When the second party started, Father Serra said good-by to his friend, Father Palou. He said he would write to him from Alta California. Father Palou promised to keep a record of all that happened.

"The day will come when those in California will want to know these things," said Father Palou.

It was May when the second land party started. Governor Portolá and Father Serra were with this group. Both were men of courage. Both were going to be very important to the story of California. Portolá was to be governor of Alta California. Father Serra would be head of the missions. Portolá was told to go as far north as Monterey. There he would build a presidio, or fort. Later a mission would be built.

20

Memory garden at Mission San Fernando

Father Serra wore the gray robe that all the Franciscans wore. His belt was a knotted rope. On his feet were heavy sandals. He wore a wide felt hat to protect him on sunny days. He used a wooden pole to help him in walking. He limped as he walked, but rarely rested. The march was painful to his leg, and Father Serra could barely stand the pain. He asked a mule driver to treat the sore just as he did those on mules. Some tallow was melted and mixed with juice from a plant. This was placed on Father Serra's leg. Next day he was able to go on.

It must have seemed a long time before Father Serra and Portolá came to San Diego Bay. They had traveled four hundred miles in forty-eight days. They were happy to see their ships with folded sails in the blue harbor. Here and there they met Indians. The Indians were surprised at all they saw. They had seen the white sails of the ships come into the harbor. They had seen Father Crespi come with the cows and mules and men. Now Father Serra and his party had come. The Indians had never seen such things before! In return for gifts, the Indians showed the newcomers where to find water.

It was July, 1769, when all four parties met on the shore of San Diego Bay. They were glad to be together in this strange new land. Father Serra and Father Crespi talked sadly together. They told of their hard trips. The *San Carlos* had had trouble on the way. The *San Antonio* had left later but came to San Diego first. The food was almost gone. The water was bad. A third of all those who came had died. Many others were sick. They were all tired and hungry.

Father Serra had courage. He did not want to turn back to Mexico. Instead he gave a prayer of thanks. He was glad they were in this new land. Those who were here could begin the work in Alta California. They must succeed!

NORTH TO MONTEREY *Portolá's search for the lost bay*

CAPTAIN PORTOLÁ knew that his journey had just begun. He must go north to set up the red and yellow flag of Spain on the Bay of Monterey. Father Serra would found the first mission here at San Diego. He would care for the sick and make friends with the Indians. Portolá would take the strongest men with him to build a fort. Father Crespi decided to go with Portolá. He would look for places where missions could be built later. The *San Antonio* returned to Mexico for more supplies and men.

Portolá's party had to follow the coast closely. That was the only way that bays could be found. At some places the mountains came down to the sea. Then the party went inland through canyons. Once they turned inland to where Mission San Juan Capistrano was founded later. They stopped by the River of Earthquakes. This was the spot where Mission San Gabriel was later built. Seventeen days away from San Diego, Father Crespi wrote in his record, "We came to a valley with a beautiful river. There is a large plain and good land for planting. It is the best place we have seen for a mission." This place is now the city of Los Angeles. No mission was ever founded there.

Portolá passed fields of wild grapes. He saw wild roses in bloom on the way. There was a place where "black pitch was boiling and bubbling." This was what we call the La Brea Tar Pits. The party marched inland through present-day San

Fernando Valley. Portolá threaded his way through a pass and came to a place we call Ventura today. From there on, along the coast, were Chumash Indians. They were the Indians of Canoe Town told about by Cabrillo. Father Crespi liked these Indians. He would remember this place and come back later.

On up the coast Portolá's party went. They passed Santa Barbara and saw more Chumash Indians. Father Crespi made a special note about this beautiful place. Now the party turned inland again. They camped at what is now San Luis Obispo. The tall Santa Lucia Mountains came down sharply to the sea. The travel was hard here. Portolá sent scouts ahead to find a better way. The scouts came back and led the party inland to a long narrow valley. This was the Salinas Valley, with a brown-colored river running through it. Now they could march north and follow the river. The river emptied into a bay. They were standing on the shore of Monterey Bay, but they did not know it. The early explorers had seen the bay from the sea. Now Portolá and his men saw it from the land side. It did not look round but seemed to be shaped like a fishhook. It was not a quiet bay. The wind made whitecaps on the waves. Where were the tall trees? Where were the friendly Indians? No rich valleys could be seen. There was no fresh water there. Only the muddy river running slowly into the bay. This could not be the beautiful bay that Vizcaíno had told about. Still, it must be close by. They would march on and see.

The party crossed another river. On the banks they found a dead bird. The soldiers called the river Pajaro ("bird") River, the name it has today. Trees were found farther north that made men look like dwarfs. Father Crespi wrote, "Here are trees so great that it takes eight men to reach around one. The wood is red and we gave them the name redwoods."

About that time in October, the fall rains began. The men were tired from marching. Rain soaked their clothes. They had almost lost courage to go on. What was the use? They certainly had not found the Bay of Monterey. Little did they

24

know it was behind them. Portolá, too, was ill and he stopped to rest. Sergeant Ortega and some scouts went ahead. Marching north, they came to a wide bay. The scouts hurried back to tell Portolá the exciting news. But Portolá was not interested. He had come to find the Bay of Monterey. His record said, "Found nothing." On the way back the party stopped at what really was Monterey Bay. A cross was put up in the sand. On it was written, "Dig at the foot and you will find a message." It read, "With no food but flour, we set out this day for San Diego . . . at the Bay of Pines, Dec. 9, 1769."

It took less than two months to get back to San Diego. Portolá told Father Serra of his trip. He had not found the Bay of Monterey. Father Serra was disappointed. He said, "Things have not gone well here either." Then he told Father Crespi and Portolá the story of San Diego.

MISSION SAN DIEGO *and how the first mission was founded*

THE FOUNDING of San Diego was not a very happy story. It was not what Father Serra expected. He had come to California to help the Indians. As he rang the bells he wondered what would happen. He turned to see if there were any Indians in sight. If there were any, they were hiding in the hills. The mission would be founded anyway. That was why he had come to Alta California. He put on his bright red-and-gold robe. He lit a candle beside the cross under the brush shelter. Then he called in a loud voice, "Come and be Christians!" Still he saw no Indians.

When the Indians did come, they were warlike. The Spaniards could not understand their language. They could only guess what the Indians were saying. They would not take food, but they liked the gifts of bright beads. When the gifts were gone, the Indians began to take other things they wanted. Soldiers fired guns into the air to scare them. They were not hurt and only laughed. One day, however, an Indian was killed. Others were hurt. They were not friendly after that.

26

Five bells still ring at Mission San Diego

It was nearly a year before any Indian came to the new mission. No Indian had even been baptized. Finally one Indian child was brought. Father Serra put a piece of bright cloth around the baby. He was about to baptize the child. Then the Indian father grabbed the child and ran off into the hills.

This was the story Father Serra told to Crespi and Portolá when they came back from their trip to the north. Father Serra still had hope. But Portolá's hopes were gone. He wanted to go back to Lower California. The *San Antonio* had not come back with supplies.

Portolá said to Father Serra, "If the supply ship does not come back soon, we will march back."

Father Serra replied, "You may go, but Father Crespi and I will stay."

They agreed on a day when they would go if no ship came. It was the evening of the last day. Suddenly someone shouted, "A sail!" The *San Antonio* had come at last!

Now that men and supplies had come, Portolá started north again by land. Father Serra wanted to go this time. He and Father Crespi decided to go on the *San Antonio*. Padre Jayme and another padre were left at San Diego. They soon found that the land by the mission was not good for growing crops. The mission was moved up the river to a place six miles away. A tall palm tree marks the place of the first mission building. The sign on it says, "First palm planted in California —1769, by Father Serra."

About a year later nearly a hundred Indians were living at the mission. No one thought there was any danger. But one night hundreds of warlike Indians came with clubs and bows and arrows. They came quietly into the church and took the padres' robes. Then they yelled and set fire to the church and all the other buildings. Before many minutes, every building was on fire. Padre Jayme came out of one of the burning buildings. He did not think that the Indians would harm him. But the

Indians dragged him to a spot near the river. Next day his friends found that the Indians had shot him with arrows. Father Serra was in Monterey when he heard the news. He was sad but not discouraged. He believed the Indians would become friendly later, and that San Diego Mission would grow.

Father Serra was right. Mission San Diego did grow. The crops were large. The first mission grapes brought by the padres were planted. Soon clusters of green and purple grapes hung heavy on the vines. The olive trees gave them all the olive oil that was needed. A new padre, Father Lasuén, came from Mexico. He was put in charge. He was a wise and able padre. He, too, traveled thousands of miles on the mission trails. Later he was to found nine of the missions of California.

Years later, when Mexico took California from the Spanish, Indians were given mission lands. Some of the Indians stayed, but most of them left. The mission was sold and fell into ruins. Then there were no more gardens and orchards.

Mission San Diego has been rebuilt since then. Five bells still ring from the tall bell tower. Some of the olive trees are still there. A wooden cross marks the spot near the mission where Father Jayme was killed. On Presidio Hill in San Diego, there is a large cross on which are these words:

"Here Father Serra first raised the cross. Here began the first mission, here the first town, San Diego. July 16, 1769."

There on Presidio Hill, which overlooks the ocean and San Diego Bay, was taken the first daring step in the adventure of settling California.

Founded
June 3, 1770

MISSION SAN CARLOS *Father Serra's home*

THE STORY of the second mission is really the story of the finding of Monterey. Once again, Portolá came to the place he had seen before. This time he felt sure he had found the Bay of Monterey. It was springtime and flowers were in bloom everywhere. The bay was quiet and blue. Twisted cypress stood near sandy beaches. Monterey in June was wonderful!

Father Serra and the *San Antonio* had not arrived. For a week Portolá waited. He had guns fired by day and signal fires burned at night to guide them to the bay. Then one night the boom of a cannon was heard. The *San Antonio* rounded the Point of Pines and anchored in the bay. Father Serra was happy to have found the Bay of Monterey, the bay round like an "O."

A presidio, or fort, where the soldiers could live, was started nearby. The soldiers would protect the mission against warlike Indians or an enemy country. Portolá raised the Spanish flag and said that now California belonged to Spain.

30

Old stone bell tower — Mission San Carlos today

After a few days Father Serra looked around carefully. "The soil here is not good for gardens," he said to Father Crespi. "No," replied Father Crespi, "and there is no stream to water the gardens. Later we will have to grow lots of food." The two padres decided that the mission should be in the beautiful Carmel Valley not far away. There they could plant beans, corn, and wheat. Cattle and horses could be raised. It was a place that pleased Father Serra, for there were trees, a river, and a lovely little bay. He wanted to make the mission here the head of all the missions that would be founded.

During the days that followed, everyone was busy in the Carmel Valley. Soon the padres and soldiers and Indians were all working together. Father Serra was the busiest one of all. He was making plans for founding other new missions up and down the California coast. He left Mission San Carlos to found Mission San Antonio, but he soon came back to help. He was proud as he watched the adobe walls grow higher! All mission buildings were to be built much like this one. They were to be made in the shape of a hollow square. All the rooms were to open out on the square, or patio.

Father Serra walked hundreds of miles up and down California. He did not think of his lameness but of those he might help on the way. When he came back from one of his trips he found his friend, Father Palou, had come from Mexico. Once again the three friends, Father Serra, Father Crespi, and Father Palou, were together. They remembered the days when they had been together in the university.

A fine stone church was not built at San Carlos until Father Lasuén came years later. He made the mission church into a beautiful building. He sent for a stone-mason to help the Indians with the work. Up went the walls of yellow stone! There were two towers and a star window on the front. Around the square by the church were the storerooms for grain and tallow. Rooms for the padres were a part of the square.

32

Each morning at sunrise and at sunset the bells in the big tower were rung. It was a call for the Indians to come to church. On special days hundreds of candles were lighted. There were no seats in the church. Women and girls sat on the floor on one side. Men and boys sat on the other side. There were many services and many busy days at Mission San Carlos. Padres from all the other missions came there with their reports. Visitors were always welcome.

One day a black ship sailed into the Bay of Monterey. No one knew the flag on it. Word went out that it was the ship of the pirate Bouchard! Governor Solá of California, sent out orders. Soldiers were to watch along the coast. Cattle and sheep were to be driven inland. Pirates must not find them. People were to take the things they valued most and bury them. Treasures from the church were to be taken inland away from the coast. Women and children must be ready to leave the mission. By night, oxcarts were creaking along the road. The pirates came to San Carlos, but they found very little to take back to their ships.

Then in the year 1834, a messenger came to the mission from Mexico. The same news came to all the missions that year. "California now belongs to Mexico," the message said. Mexico made a new law about the California missions. It said that the padres must leave the missions. If they stayed they could no longer care for the land or the workshops. The Indians might stay and have some of the mission land and cattle. Some of the early California settlers were not honest. Land was taken away from the Indians. They did not understand what was happening. Soon they had no homes, no land, no cattle. Some went to work on the ranchos. Some went back to the hills to live as they had before mission days. Most of the things they had learned from the padres were forgotten.

Mission San Carlos was offered for sale. No one cared to buy it. Only one padre was left to care for the few Indians who were still there. He was a cheerful man who always carried apples in the sleeves of his robe for the children. Then one day he left too. The mission buildings were left alone. The roof of the church fell in. Birds nested in the ruins. There the church stood for years until it was rebuilt.

One of the old bells still hangs in the bell tower at Mission San Carlos. The famous star window is in the front tower. One room shows how a mission kitchen looked. On the north side of the buildings is the room where Padre Serra lived and died. A small wooden cross marks his grave in the chapel. Padre Serra left San Carlos many times to carry on his mission building. But it was the place where he always liked to return. You, too, may see the mission in the wooded hills of the Carmel Valley where Father Serra had his home.

Founded
July 14, 1771

MISSION SAN ANTONIO DE PADUA *and its busy daily life*

ONE DAY Father Junípero Serra left his mission at San Carlos. He thought there was need for another mission. He was happy as he walked along the dusty road with some of his good friends. He was glad that the work was going well in Alta California. He was even happier that they had decided not to turn back that day in San Diego!

They came to a wild valley in the Santa Lucia Mountains. It was full of oaks and had a stream running through it. As Father Serra was hanging the bells on an oak, he looked up and saw an Indian. That same day other Indians came, too, and brought the padres gifts of pine nuts and seeds.

The mission did not start well, though. The first harvest failed. The river went dry. The padres had not counted on rivers that were full of water in the winter and dry in the summer. They moved the mission three miles away and began again. This time they dug ditches to carry the water to the mission and the fields.

35

The Indians were surprised at the tools the padres used for building. The padres showed the Indians how to make adobe bricks. All of the missions made them in the same way. First the Indian dug a place in the ground like a shallow bowl. Clay was pounded until it was fine and smooth. The clay was then thrown into the pit or bowl. Water was brought from a ditch and poured on the clay. Dry grasses or straw were mixed with the mud. Then one of the Indians stepped into the adobe mud. With his bare feet he mixed the mud and straw together. Then the mud was put into wooden molds twelve inches square and four inches thick, After the adobe had partly dried, the mold was taken off. The mud bricks were left in the hot summer sun until they were dry and hard. Then the bricks were ready to be made into a wall.

Many bricks had to be made for the new mission church. A small house was built for the padre. Houses were built for shops. Large houses had to be made to store grain and other crops. Near the mission buildings were small huts for the Indians. Each family had its own place to live. The Indian girls lived at the mission until they married. Padres and Indians worked together until the mission and all the buildings were done.

It was not long before many Indians came to live in the little houses by the mission. But there were others who did not. They did not like the Indians to give up their old ways. They planned an attack on the mission. They did little harm, but after that the padres worked harder than ever. They planted a large pear orchard and an olive orchard. Soon Mission San Antonio had wonderful pears shining in the sun! No one had ever seen such large pears!

The grain crops were good too. One of the padres had an idea. Why not build a water mill for grinding grain into flour? The Indians did not understand how water could grind corn and wheat. The large stone mill ground slowly, but it ground good flour. Soon all the missions heard what fine flour Mission San Antonio had.

Mission San Antonio became famous for something else. Golden-colored horses were raised at the mission. They were called palominos. They were used in the parades on festival days. Everyone liked them and wanted them.

Like all the rest of the missions, though, there was trouble ahead for Mission San Antonio. There came the word from Mexico that the missions were to be given up. It was not long after that the Indians were gone. Only a few people came to San Antonio to walk through the lonely church and orchards and gardens.

Today it is interesting to turn off the main highway near King City to see the mission. It was not easy for the padres to build a mission in such a faraway spot with no one but Indians to help. Mission San Antonio still stands alone in the warm, broad valley. When it was rebuilt there was a big celebration. Many visitors came to the services and the fiesta. Now San Antonio has become a "living mission." Padres live and work there as they used to do. Trades and arts are taught to young men. Water will be brought from the old creek by the mill. Once again the mission is as it was when the padres and Indians left it in the valley of the oaks near the Santa Lucia Mountains.

Mission San Antonio

Founded
September 8, 1771

MISSION SAN GABRIEL *and the largest grapevine*

MISSION SAN GABRIEL was founded near a river. It was called "Rio de los Temblores" or "The River of Earthquakes." The site had just been chosen when a group of Indians came. They were armed with bows and arrows. Something had to be done to show them that the padres had come to help them. One of the padres thought of a beautiful picture he had. He unrolled it before them. The Indians stopped their yelling and turned to look in wonder. Some of them placed strings of beads in front of the picture. It was a sign to the padres that they wished to be at peace. Many more Indians came to see the picture. They brought food with them and became friends. The padres gave them corn. They buried it in the ground. Soon it sprouted! "White man's magic," they said.

For a while those who lived at the mission had to depend on food from supply boats. Sometimes the boats did not come and people went hungry. As soon as possible they started farming. When they did, they found that San Gabriel was a

40

The famous bell wall of Mission San Gabriel still stands

wonderful place for crops. It was not long before fields of grain could be seen on all sides of the mission. When it turned golden, the Indians carried it from the fields. A level piece of ground was cleared. This ground was called the threshing ground. The ground was pounded until it was hard and smooth. The grain from the field was spread over the ground. Horses were driven round and round over it.

42

The hoofs of the galloping horses broke the wheat stalks into small pieces. The grains of wheat fell off the stems. Then the women tossed the grain from their baskets into the air. The wind blew the pieces away and left only the grain. After the harvest, there was a special service. Some of the Indians made a cross of two poles. The poles were wrapped with the golden wheat stalks. One man carried this cross of ripe wheat high in the air. The others followed him, marching together

and singing. They marched to the church. The bells rang gaily. The marching men and women and children all sang a song of thanksgiving. They were glad for the good harvest. Then the cross of wheat was carried into the church and put where everyone could see it.

Mission San Gabriel became one of the richest missions. At one time there were nearly eight thousand neophytes or mission Indians there. The mission had thousands of cattle and horses. They were branded with the letter "T" that stood for *temblores,* or earthquakes. Sometimes four hundred cattle were killed in a week to feed the Indian neophytes.

Each year in the spring, there was great excitement at the mission. It was time for the journey for salt *(jornada para sal)* to start. Enough food had to be taken to last a month. The oxen were yoked to the old wooden *carretas.* The journey to the desert was slow and hot and there were no roads. At last the men saw the bright white fields of salt in a very low valley. On the way back the *carretas* creaked with the heavy load. There was enough salt for the mission and the nearby pueblo of Los Angeles to last for another year.

The year of 1812 was a year of earthquakes. Many mission walls and towers crumbled to the ground that year. San Gabriel's tower fell to the ground with a loud crash! The padres dug the bells out of the fallen stones. They built a new tower on the other end of the church, and once again the bells rang.

San Gabriel Mission had many happy days to remember. Then orders came that the mission was to be sold. The Indians did not want to stay there after the padres were gone. There was no one to care for the fields any more. The mission church was left empty.

Today all the mission Indians are gone. The ranches are all gone too. The lands of the mission are now covered by southern California cities. The fine old church still stands. It does not look like any of the others. At one end is the bell tower just as it used to be. At the other end is a stairway. Here the Indians used to go up to the choir room to sing. There is much left to tell the story of San Gabriel Mission. There is an old grapevine that was planted in mission days. It is now almost as large as a city block. Part of the cactus hedge is left. It once kept animals out of the gardens. An old tile canal has been found that came from an old mill (El Molino) several miles away. Traffic now speeds past the doors of the mission. There are modern buildings all around it. Inside the thick adobe walls of the church it is dim and quiet. People may still worship there as the padres and Indians did one hundred and fifty years ago.

*Founded
September 1, 1772*

MISSION SAN LUIS OBISPO *and the serape weavers*

ON ONE OF HIS TRIPS Father Serra came to a valley where Portolá once camped. After finding a spot for the mission, he looked around the valley. Some of the ground had been torn up by bears. The bears had been looking for roots to eat. The soldiers killed some of the bears and called the place the Valley of the Bears. When there was little food later, those who lived at the mission were glad the bears were there. For three months they shot them for food. It was good that they did, for the other missions could give Mission San Luis Obispo very little. They could give only fifty pounds of flour, some wheat seed, a little chocolate, and a small box of sugar. But Mission San Luis Obispo had enough bear meat to share with Monterey.

When the Indians heard the bears had been killed, they became friendly with the padres. The Indians had always been afraid of the bears. They could not kill them with their arrows. Now the bears were gone and the white men had helped

46

Mission San Luis Obispo today

the Indians. The next thing was to plant seed for crops. But it was some time before the padres knew how to farm in California. What kind of crops would grow? When was the rainy season? They planted in winter. Floods came and seed was lost. In summer the fields dried out. Now they had learned about the long dry summer and the wet winter. Seed had to be planted at the right time of the year. Crops had to have water. When the padres and Indians learned these things, all had plenty to eat.

The first adobe buildings at the mission had roofs of dry tule grass. The Indians who had not come to live at the mission decided to burn the buildings. They put a burning wick on an arrow and shot it at the tule roofs. In a few minutes the roofs were red with fire. Three different times they did the same thing. Finally the padres thought of a way to protect the roofs. They showed the helpers how to make tiles. Sand was dusted over a log and then clay put on the sand. With clean fingers they smoothed the top of the clay. After tiles were dried in the sun, they were baked in the fire until red. Now the new tile roofs of Mission San Luis Obispo were safe from fire. Soon the other missions heard about the tiles. They began making clay tiles too.

Sheep had come over the long trail from Lower California. Soon there were large flocks. The Indians took care of them. The sheep gave them wool for clothing. Indians learned to be careful shepherds. They took the sheep where there were grass and fresh water. The Indians kept them safe from wild animals. In the spring the heavy wool was cut off. The wool was put into large hide bags. In the mission work-shops it was washed and combed. The Indian women spun wool into yarn. Both men and women then wove it into cloth. They used heavy wool blankets to cover them at night. They wore smaller blankets like a coat. This was called a serape. It had an opening in the center. The serape was put over the head, and it hung down back and front. A light kind of wool cloth was woven called *jerga*.

Mission Indians cared for crops this way

This cloth was used to make clothing. A man wore loose trousers and shirt. A woman wore a skirt and blouse. Indians were always busy making serapes and clothes. The other missions were glad to buy them from San Luis Obispo.

There came a time when there were no longer peace and happiness at the mission. Mexico sent word that California now belonged to Mexico. The Californians were surprised, but they were not worried. The mission padres were disturbed by the news. The Mexicans thought Father Martinez, one of the padres at San Luis Obispo, was loyal to Spain. They were about to send·him to Mexico for trial. He begged not to go, and so was sent to Spain. From Spain he wrote to his friends telling them how much he missed his "Little San Luis." Finally word came that all the padres were to give up the missions. By this time the padres had been working in the California missions for fifty years. The government of Mexico said that was too long. By then the Indians should be able to take care of themselves. This was called "secularization." A man was sent to each mission to close it and divide the land and cattle and sell the mission. The Indians were given a small share of land and some cattle. Some of them did not know what to do with the land. Many were glad to go back to their old ways. It was the same in all the missions during this time, from the year 1830 to 1840.

Mission San Luis Obispo was sold. When it was finally returned to the Church, it was rebuilt. The large front door is the one used in the old mission days. It hangs on the same old iron hinges. Father Serra used the baptismal bowl that is still in the mission. One of the first tiles is there, and you can see the fingerprints on it. The gardens are filled with flowers of many kinds and colors. Each year a fiesta is held to celebrate the founding of the mission. A barbecue dinner is served from the padre's kitchen. Thousands come to visit and see the old mission. Mission San Luis Obispo is the halfway place in the mission chain. Visitors like to think of the old days when it stood alone in the "Valley of the Bears."

Large flocks of sheep such as this were important in mission days

MISSION SAN FRANCISCO *and how it traded with ships*

ONE RAINY SUNDAY afternoon after services, Father Serra and his mission friends hurried over to Monterey. They wanted to welcome a brave soldier, Colonel Juan de Anza. He had come with more than two hundred people from Mexico. The party had crossed a thousand miles of desert and mountains. They had come to found a new colony, a fort, and a mission for Spain. With the padres, they journeyed northward. On a high hill they looked over the blue water of the largest bay they had ever seen. This was a perfect place for a fort, they thought. A fort here would help to keep the people of other countries out of California. It would be a wonderful bay where trading ships could come. Back of the hills, Colonel de Anza and the padres came to a little stream and a small lake. They named the stream Dolores. The mission that was built there later was sometimes called Mission Dolores.

The settlers quickly put up many little brush huts. The *San Carlos* had not yet

52

The church is all that remains of Mission San Francisco

come with supplies, but friendly Indians saw that the people had enough to eat. They were glad to trade wild red berries for red beads. In return for knives and bright pieces of cloth, they gave the settlers fish. The settlers were happy to make friends with the Indians. Father Serra was even happier. He liked to work with Indians such as these. He was happy, too, that the sixth mission was to be founded by this great harbor. Now St. Francis, the first Franciscan, could be honored. While Father Serra was on a visit to Mexico, Father Palou founded Mission San Francisco.

Father Serra asked his old friend, Father Palou, to stay and take charge. The few Indians who came to the mission liked Father Palou. They were willing to help him, but it was a long time before building started. The mission lands were small and there was not enough room for crops. The climate was foggy and windy. Some of the Indians from inland could not get used to the colder climate.

When the *San Carlos* did come, it brought gifts and supplies. Carpenters and sailors from the ship came to help with the new buildings. Ship's carpenters made the heavy carved wooden doors.

Father Serra, who had gone back to Mission San Carlos, could hardly wait to see the finished buildings. One day he made a surprise visit. He was sixty-three years old, but he walked all the way. It was the feast day of St. Francis, and he wanted to be there for a special service. He was pleased with the fine church. So were the others who came. They liked the beautiful carved doors and the red tile roof.

The mission lands around San Francisco were not very good for crops. But missions to the south raised lots of cattle. Hides and tallow from these missions were sent to Mission San Francisco and traded with trading ships that came to California. It took many weeks to get the hides ready. They were soaked in lime water to make them soft. Then it was easy to scrape off the hair with a sharp piece of iron. A patient Indian staked the hide to the ground to stretch it. After the hides were dry, they could be stacked into a *carreta* ready to go to the harbor.

54

At first only Spanish ships were allowed to trade with the Californians. But it was not long before Yankee American traders came in their boats to California. They, too, found they could make money by selling hides and tallow. They went up and down the coast until their boats were loaded. Only then could they start back. Each hide was worth about two dollars. They were sometimes called "leather dollar bills."

It was a very exciting day when a trading ship came in. Every Spaniard and Indian who could be spared from work went to the boat. Many old *carretas* could be seen on the road leading to the harbor. They groaned under the heavy load of hides and tallow bags. After the hides were counted the captain told the people to come aboard and trade. The deck of the ship looked just like a store. Women wanted ribbons and shawls and silks and cottons for skirts. They also wanted fans and beads, combs and laces. Soldiers went away from the trading ship with uniforms and gunpowder. Padres came to the ships to get pictures and robes to be used in the church. Men took home shoes and tools and fishhooks. Everyone looked forward to trading day on the ships!

At last the climate proved too cold and foggy for most of the Indians at the mission. They were taken across the bay to the sunny valley of San Rafael. Only a few old people and some children were left. Women had to do men's work. Father Palou spent his time writing books. One was about Father Serra's life. Another was the story of the California Indians.

About this time Father Palou was sent word from Mexico that the mission church was to be closed. In the meantime, a little village had grown up between the presidio and the mission. When gold was found inland, the village became an important city. St. Francis was honored again, for it was called San Francisco. Gold seekers came and stayed on the mission land. White tents were seen everywhere. On Saturday nights there were dances in the rooms of the mission. On Saturday

afternoons there were bear and bullfights on the mission grounds.

Many changes have come since Mission San Francisco was founded. Today the charming church looks much as it did when Father Palou was there. The other parts of the mission buildings are gone. Like Mission San Gabriel, it has become crowded into a small space. It is now just a part of the great city by San Francisco Bay.

Founded
November 1, 1776

MISSION SAN JUAN CAPISTRANO
and the great stone church

WHEN CAPTAIN PORTOLÁ first passed through a certain valley of southern California, he had written, "This is a most inviting valley. It has trees and lots of water. It has so many wild grapevines that it looks like a vineyard!"

Nearby was a village of fifty Indians. Their bodies were covered with red and yellow paint. Into this valley Father Serra sent Father Lasuén to found a mission. The bells were hung on a frame and rung. The chapel and a few brush houses were made. Suddenly a horseman came riding at great speed. He quickly told the story of the Indian attack on San Diego. The bells were taken down and buried in the ground. The mission could not be founded for a while. Father Lasuén and his companions hurried to San Diego to see if they could help. All that was left were the little huts and a wooden cross.

A year passed by. The grass had grown tall around the cross when Father Serra came with others to begin the mission. The bells were dug out of the earth. The

58

The charming gardens at San Juan Capistrano

Indians were glad to have the padres back. After the mission was founded, Father Serra walked back to San Gabriel Mission. He wanted to get others to come south and help in the building. Then he went back to his mission home in Monterey.

At first a small adobe church was built at Mission San Juan Capistrano. Father Serra used to come there for special services. It is still called Father Serra's church, and it is the oldest church in California. Later it was decided to build a fine stone church. There had to be many Indians to help. Everyone wanted to have a part in the work. About four miles away was a place where there were many stones. The men loaded the large stones in clumsy *carretas,* and brought them to the mission. Some of the stones were dragged with chains. The women wanted to help too. They carried nets filled with smaller stones on their backs. Even the children put small stones in sacks. Day after day they went back and forth on the trail. Looking down from the hilltop, the padres could see two lines of Indians. Back and forth they went from mission to quarry. They sang and chattered as they carried the heavy loads. A fine stone builder came to help build the church. It had six round domes. The bell towers could be seen for ten miles. The bells could be heard even farther. Money was needed to pay for some of the things in the church. A weaver was brought to the mission. He taught the Indians to weave blankets and carpets of bright colors. These were used for trade with the ships. Hides were made into fine saddles and sold.

The mission patio was a place where people worked and played. They made everything that was needed by the Indians and padres. In the patio was the blacksmith who did the ironwork. The soapmaker had his kettles there. The carpenters were at work there too. Near the patio were basins of stone where the hides were soaked. Saddle makers sat nearby, cutting and sewing the leather. Women sat under the arches and ground corn and acorns into meal. The girls did spinning and weaving. Bullfights were held in the plaza, but there was a bull game that was

played in the patio. A sack of silver was tied between a bull's horns. Then the men tried to grab the sack of money. The Indian women and children sat on the roofs around the patio and watched the men chase the bull.

Finally, when the buildings were all done, there was a big celebration. It was the biggest one ever held in the early days of California. The governor came in his fine suit of black and gold. The soldiers came in bright red uniforms. The Indians had worked hard for this day! When the sun went down there was a gay fiesta.

There were unhappy days at the mission too. First there was a small earthquake. Later two roofs were burned. No rain came for the crops. One night an Indian boy was trying to kill bats. He was carrying a lighted candle. The candle fell and set fire to the storerooms that were filled with tallow, wheat, and corn. Only gray ashes were left.

One winter day in December, 1812, there was a morning service in the great stone church. The people heard a loud roar. Was it the sound of guns or the sea? The tower seemed to move. The walls swayed back and forth. In fright, everyone looked up at the domes. They opened wide enough for the light to come in. A second shock sent the bell tower crashing down on the roof. The front door could not be opened. When the earthquake was over, forty Indians were buried under the stones. The church ended after only nine years!

The first Mexican governor of California sent word that the mission was to be sold. Stones and tiles were taken away. Iron kettles were taken out of the soap and tallow vats. Even Father Serra's church was used as a storehouse for wool and grains until the roof fell in. After fifty years, Father O'Sullivan came to California for his health. He set up his cot among the walls. He grew stronger in the warm sunshine. As he became better he began to clean up the ruins. The bell ringer helped him take away the weeds. Together they planted flowers in the garden. Father O'Sullivan was able to get money to build Father Serra's little church again.

The great sandstone church is still in ruins. This is the part of the mission built of stones by the Indians. It was such a large church the padres never tried to build it again. Climbing vines and roses cover the old ruins. White doves splash in the water of the mossy fountains. Services are held in the little chapel of Father Serra. Between the little church and the ruins is the bell wall. The bells have hung there since the earthquake. Behind the buildings may be seen the old stone basins where the hides were fixed and the tallow and soap were made.

Every year in the spring, about March 19, St. Joseph's Day, thousands of people come to Mission San Juan Capistrano to welcome the swallows. The swallows have come every year on this day for as long as people can remember. They build their mud nests in the cracks and under the roofs and arches. They fill the charming gardens with their happy notes and seem to be glad to return to their mission again. When the first chill days of fall come about St. John's Day in October, the swallows leave for the winter. All is quiet in the mission garden again.

Founded
January 12, 1777

MISSION SANTA CLARA *and its famous fruits*

EIGHT YEARS had passed since Portolá's march into Alta California. On that march he had taken his company through the Santa Clara Valley. He called it the Plain of Oaks. Now the padres had come to found a mission in this valley not far south of San Francisco. A few months after the mission was founded, the pueblo of San Jose began. Spanish people built houses and marked out their fields. They called their town El Pueblo de San Jose. Pueblo is the Spanish name for town.

At first there were only three Indians to help build, dig, and plow. No one else came to help the padres build a church. It was lucky that the other buildings were plain and small. Before long the winter rains almost washed the mud walls away.

"This place is too low. We must move away from here before the rains come again!" said one of the padres.

The mission was built again in a safer place. Father Serra came to lay the first

64

Mission Santa Clara is now part of Santa Clara University

brick of the new building. This time there were more Indians to help. When the church was done, Father Serra came to make his last visit there. He was now old, but he wanted to see the fine pictures in the new mission church. Indians had gone miles to get red rock dust. The dust had been mixed with cactus juice to make paint. Father Serra was pleased with the pictures the Indians had made. It was worth the long walk from Monterey just to see the bright pictures on the walls, he said.

Because of sickness among them, many of the Indians in the valley did not come to the mission.

"We will go to the Indian villages and baptize them there," said the padre.

After that the Indians were friendly. Before long two thousand were living at the mission. There were more Indians baptized here than at any other mission. Soon green gardens and orchards spread as far as you could see. From the start this valley was a perfect garden spot! The fruits from the orchards became famous all over California. There were enough pears and plums and peaches to share with the other missions nearby.

One day the supply ship, *San Antonio,* came into Monterey Bay. There was always excitement when a ship came into the harbor. That day there was a special reason for the excitement that seemed to fill the air! Two bells had come from Spain. The King of Spain had sent them to Mission Santa Clara. It was not often that a king sent bells to a mission! It was hard to get the bells off the boat and into an oxcart. At last they were brought safely to Santa Clara. Then the Indians gathered to hear the sweet sound of the bells as they rang together.

"There is one thing that we must remember," said the padre. "We have promised that these bells must ring at eight-thirty every night!"

About this time Father Catalá was sent to have charge of the mission. He noticed that the people in the nearby pueblo of San Jose did not like to go to church. To be sure, the pueblo was four miles away from the church!

66

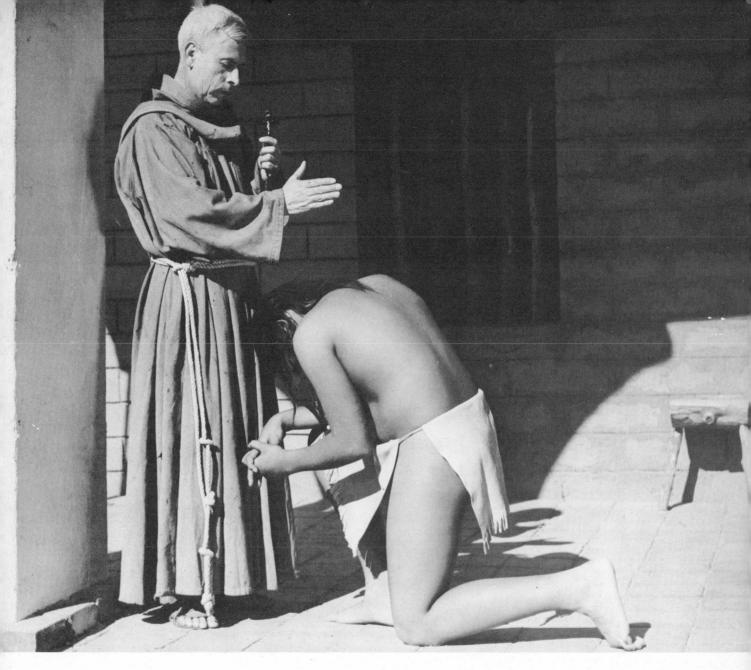

A Padre blessing an Indian — a scene typical of mission days

"Perhaps I can help these people," said Father Catalá. "Maybe they will come to the mission if we build a road right up to the door of the church."

A long straight road was built from San Jose to the mission. It was called the "Beautiful Way," or Alameda. Three rows of trees were planted on each side. Then the travelers did not have to walk in the summer sun. Even this seemed to do no good, for very few came from the pueblo to the mission. Then the pueblo built a church of its own.

In the year of 1812 there were earthquakes. Santa Clara Mission was almost destroyed, as many others were that year. A mission was started at another place not far away. Many of the adobes and tiles of the old building were used in the new one.

Finally Santa Clara received the same news that the other missions did. Word came from Mexico that the padres were to leave the mission churches. No Indians stayed to care for the land. The orchards and gardens that once were so green became brown and dry. Fruit fell from the trees for lack of water. The buildings were not cared for any more. Many settlers were coming to live in that part of California. No houses could be found, so many of them crowded into the mission buildings.

One day a Jesuit priest arrived from Oregon. He was sent by the Church to find a good place for a school. People who were living in the mission were driven out. Other teachers came to help him start California's first college. The teachers sat on old tree trunks in the garden. The twelve students who came sat under the grapevines on wooden benches. One day fire destroyed the church. The tower with its bells plunged down. One of the King's bells was cracked. The other bell was dragged from the fallen ruins. At eight-thirty that night it rang again as always. More students came to the college. It became so large that new buildings had to be added.

There is little of the old mission left today. Only the storeroom and some old walls stand. But the church has been made to look like the old mission church building. The gardens are even more beautiful than they were in the early days. For almost one hundred and fifty years the bells have rung each evening just as the King of Spain wished.

Founded
March 31, 1782

MISSION SAN BUENAVENTURA
and how the Indians became farmers

SAN BUENAVENTURA was the ninth and last mission founded by Father Serra. For fourteen years he had worked in his California missions. Many, many times he had walked the long way from San Diego to Monterey. All the years had not been easy. But he had always been happy in his work in California. Now he was seventy years old. He wished to visit his missions once more. He wanted to see the padres and his Indian friends. Then he came back to San Carlos, the place he called home. Soon after his return, he was buried beside his friend, Father Crespi. Indians brought hundreds of wild flowers to put on his grave.

Father Lasuén carried on the building of Mission San Buenaventura. The Chumash Indians did most of the work. This tribe was famous for its woodwork and baskets. They made the best boats in California at that time. These canoes were strong enough to go out to the islands and back.

The Franciscan padres were California's first farmers. At San Buenaventura,

70

The church is all that remains of Mission San Buenaventura

the padres worked hard to plant vegetables and grains. The soil was good, but there was not much water and the Indians did not know how to plant. More than once they had to hunt and fish for enough to eat. After the fall rains, when the ground was soft, it was planted. Seed was scattered by hand. The warm California sunshine made the seeds sprout quickly. Fruit trees were planted in the mission gardens. The Indians thought of the time when they had to dig roots and gather wild berries. That was in the days before the mission. But now there was plenty to eat for all.

The padres also taught the Indians to dam up the water and build canals. San Buenaventura was sometimes called "the place of canals." One of the canals was seven miles long! After that the gardens were always green. Vegetables that grew there were better than any yet seen. The English explorer, Captain Vancouver, made a visit to the mission. He wrote, "Nowhere have I seen such gardens! They are dreams of wealth and beauty!" He took back to the ship with him as many vegetables as twenty mules could carry!

San Buenaventura, too, felt the earthquake of 1812. Cracks were made in the adobe walls. While the Indians watched, part of a wall of the church fell down. The single tower swayed to and fro with a clatter of bells. Then a second quake was felt. The ocean came up so high that it almost reached the mission.

The buildings were rebuilt. This time the Indians made sure the walls were strong. Everyone had settled down to live peacefully again. Then one night a messenger came galloping down the dusty road on his fast horse. He shouted, "Bouchard, the pirate, is coming! He is coming to rob our towns and our missions!" The padres told everyone in the mission to get ready to leave. Robes of the padres were folded and laid away carefully. Holes were dug in the fields to bury the statues. The crosses and candlesticks were put in baskets. Food and grain were put in baskets too. Then the baskets were strapped over the backs of mules. All were ready to leave if the pirates came. They were going over the mountains away from

72

the coast. "Ah! That will teach that pirate Bouchard a lesson," the padre said. "If he comes here, he will find nothing!"

The pirates did come to Santa Barbara, north of San Buenaventura. When they got there, they were scared away. Bouchard's black ship was not seen again. The people came back and unpacked their things. San Buenaventura was saved this time!

Years later a messenger brought other alarming news. The news said that California had become a part of Mexico. Down came the red and gold flag of Spain. It had flown over California since the time of Portolá more than fifty years before. Up went the green, white, and red flag of Mexico. The padres said, "What will happen next? Who will own the missions and the lands?" Everyone wondered. Then the worst news came. Mexico had made new laws for California. One law was that the missions would be closed. The padres were to leave the churches. After the padres were gone, most of the Indians left too. The fields they once had been so proud of became bare and brown.

When the railroad was built nearby, a town grew up around the mission. The name of San Buenaventura seemed too long. The people changed the name to Ventura. Only the mission church is left to tell us the story of early days. The mission fields have become busy city streets that crowd the church in on all sides. But the old bells still ring out from the tall bell tower, and two very old pine trees still stand in front of the mission. A sea captain once planted them so that they might be used for sailing masts someday!

MISSION SANTA BARBARA *and how the water canals were made*

PORTOLÁ once camped where Santa Barbara Mission was to be founded seventeen years later. He found many Indians living nearby. They kept Portolá and his party awake all night. They came and brought fish, acorns, baskets, and feathers. They played on strange flutes and pipes. Finally Portolá gave them beads so that they would go away and leave them alone!

Several times, also, Father Serra had walked along this beautiful trail by the sea. He always told of its beauty. He thought it was the best place of all for a mission. He never lived to see the tenth mission founded there. It was Father Lasuén who finally chose the exact spot. The mission was built on a hill with a view of the blue sea and the islands. On the altar Father Lasuén placed a little light in a red bowl. It has never gone out in more than a hundred and sixty years!

Very soon after the mission was founded the Indians came in great numbers. The padres taught them to build their own adobe houses. It was not long until

74

Mission Santa Barbara is still queen of the missions

many mission buildings were built. After that it seemed there was always building at Santa Barbara. So many Indians came that buildings had to be made larger and larger. The fourth church building is the one we see today. There was lots of yellow sandstone near the mission. It was used instead of adobe. Lime from sea shells held the blocks together.

When the buildings were finished a great celebration followed. Everyone who could come was invited. The Indians were amazed by what they saw! All the candles in the church were lighted. Flags flew and the Sunday bells were rung. Even the governor was there. The gray-robed padres put on their robes of gold-and-silver cloth. A three-day fiesta came after the services. Oxen and sheep were roasted every day for the feasts. No work was done. In the afternoon the men and boys had races and games. The evenings were the best of all! There were singing and dancing, both Indian and Spanish. The houses were made bright by the light of the fireworks!

The next task was to provide more water. There was not enough water for the mission and the gardens. A dam was built high up in the canyon. Two large stone basins were built on the hillside behind the mission. One canal went through the gardens to the pueblo of Santa Barbara. The other one ran through the mission grounds to a fountain. From there it flowed through the mouth of a carved stone bear into a smaller basin. This basin was large enough for the women to do their washing in it. On washdays the women sat by the basin with their piles of clothes, splashing, soaping, rubbing, and chatting.

Trouble was ahead for Santa Barbara Mission. Bouchard, the pirate, cast anchor in the bay. He had come from South America to steal from towns and missions along the coast. José de la Guerra was commander of the presidio, or fort. He and his soldiers thought of a plan. The small company of men marched around and around a hill. Bouchard watched from the pirate ship. He could count the number of men over and over. It looked as though a lot of men were marching. He thought there were too many for him to fight. He raised a white flag of peace before coming ashore. He traded some prisoners with Captain de la Guerra. Then he sailed away.

In the next year a great forest fire blazed on the hills not far from the mission. The mission was not hurt, but the vineyards were burned black. Then there was a year when no rain fell. Everyone cried for rain! One wished it for his corn. Another

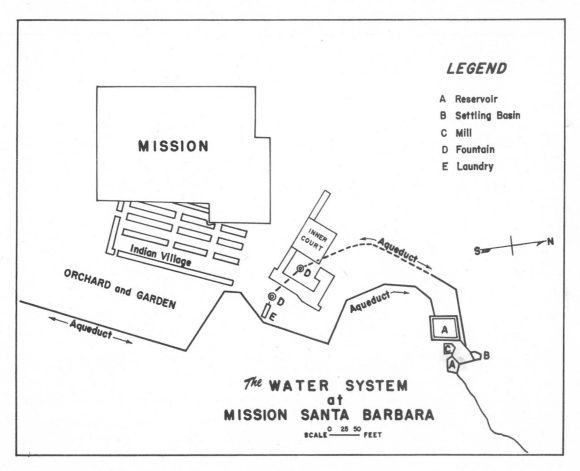

The WATER SYSTEM
at
MISSION SANTA BARBARA

LEGEND

A Reservoir
B Settling Basin
C Mill
D Fountain
E Laundry

wished it for his wheat, and all wanted it for their starving cattle. The mission padres decided to pray for rain. The padres led the people from the church to the beach, chanting and praying that rain would come. Rain came, and once again everything was green.

Word came to Mission Santa Barbara as it did to all other missions. Mexico sent orders to close the mission churches. The Indians stayed for a short time. Then Franciscan padres from other missions decided to make this mission their home. Some years later a Franciscan college was started there.

There never has been a time when the padres have not lived in the mission. They have taken care of it through all the years. Mission Santa Barbara looks almost the same today as it always has. The sandstone church is one of the finest in California. Besides the great church, there are two beautiful gardens and the rooms where the Franciscans live. The interesting early canal system may still be seen at the mission. You can trace parts of the stone aqueduct from the canyon to the fountain in the mission gardens. It was so well made that one of the basins is still used by the city of Santa Barbara.

For twenty-five years, during August, the mission bells have rung in a Fiesta of Old Spanish Days. For three days there are parades and plays, costumes and music. The fiesta begins the first evening on the steps of the mission church. A play is given by the mission fathers which tells the story of the founding of Santa Barbara Mission. The play tells about early life at the mission when the Indians were there. After the play, bells are rung and bright fireworks light up the mission gardens.

The second day there is a parade that shows the history of Santa Barbara. Flowers are given to those who line the streets along the way. Men in Spanish costumes ride on golden-colored palomino horses. The silver saddles of the horsemen are the finest in the world. In the Plaza de la Guerra there is a fruit and flower market. It is like the old Spanish market place (*El Mercado*). Singers in Spanish dresses stroll in and out among the people in the market place. At all hours there are singing and dancing in the courthouse gardens.

A careful history of Santa Barbara Mission has always been kept. During fiesta days these pages of history are on display. One may see the beautiful handwriting of Father Serra. There is a record of births made by Father Lasuén. Each year the California padres used to make a report about each mission. One report shows the number of cattle and sheep, the number of pounds of barley, corn, and beans planted. One old record shows what the mission wanted sent from Mexico. Cloth and hats, sugar and rice were needed. The order is there telling the people to leave the mission because of the coming of Bouchard, the pirate! All of these things bring back memories of old mission days.

Founded
December 8, 1787

MISSION LA PURÍSIMA *and how the Indians were taught to build*

FATHER LASUÉN, who became the president of the missions, was a great man for making plans. He wanted to explore and find the best places for the missions that were to be founded. For a long time he had planned a mission between San Luis Obispo and Santa Barbara. He liked the pleasant valley where he founded the eleventh mission. He called it Mission La Purísima Concepción.

For a while it did not seem that the place he chose was a good one. The rains were so heavy that the workers could not start to build. In the cold winter there were many hungry bears that made trouble for them. Building was started, though, just as soon as possible. Springs of water were found. The Indians helped to build dams that brought water to the new gardens.

Father Lasuén sent Father Payeras to care for the new mission. He stayed there all the rest of his life. He was made president of the missions after Father Lasuén, but he never left Mission La Purísima. He was a wise padre who kept everyone at

Today Mission La Purísima has come to life again

peace during hard times. The Chumash Indians liked him from the very first. They liked the little presents and the food that were given them. They liked the padre, who was gentle and kind to them. Soon a church and Indian huts were built.

In December, 1812, La Purísima felt the earthquake. At first the earth shook so hard the neophytes could hardly stand up. For several days more the earth shook. The buildings were thrown into ruins. The church treasures were buried under the piles of adobe bricks. In the hills behind the mission there was a big crack. Out of it came oily sand and water.

Father Payeras had to begin again, but he had great courage. He decided to move the mission four miles north on the other side of the river. Some huts were put up quickly. Some of the Indians came back again. Logs were floated down the Santa Inés River to within a mile of the mission. Then the logs were hauled the rest of the way. About this time Father Payeras, their good friend, died. After two years, only half of the buildings were finished. La Purísima was a long, narrow adobe mission with three buildings.

There were many shops at La Purísima. Indians learned all kinds of trades even though they did not go to school. The padres were kind and patient with them. They showed them how to use wood for building and carving. Some of the Indians became carpenters and blacksmiths. Some of them became good bricklayers and made strong adobe walls. Others drove oxen and mules. Still others tamed the wild cattle. They made leather from the hides. Soap and candles were made from the tallow. They pressed olives for oil and grapes for wine. Weaving was done with wool. Every day was a busy day for everyone.

Finally the mission was taken away from the padres and sold. There was the same neglect that took place in all the missions about this time. For a short while bandits lived in the mission. Later it was used as a stable and a place for sheep. At last almost all of the mission buildings were gone. Only walls with no roofs and a few pillars were left. On one wall hung part of the painted pulpit where padres had preached. Inside on the floor were piles of earth and stone. Swallows made their nests in the corners of the ruins. The mission lay all alone in the hot sun by the dry, brown hills.

Today La Purísima has come to life again! In 1935 five hundred acres of land around the mission were made into a state park. The United States put to work two hundred young men. Old plans were found and studied carefully. Everything was to be made exactly as it was when the Indians lived there. Clay was put into pits and tramped with bare feet just as the Indians had done. Bricks were made into molds. Pine beams were cut by hand. Carved chairs were made. The roof tiles were made with wooden molds. The beautiful gardens were planted as they once were. Water was brought again from a spring nearby to fountains in the gardens. Again branches of the pear trees are heavy with fine fruit! La Purísima Mission now looks exactly as Father Payeras had planned it in the beginning.

*Founded
September 25, 1791*

MISSION SANTA CRUZ *on the Bay of Monterey*

THE EARLY EXPLORERS were pleased with the northern shore of Monterey Bay. They liked the climate, the herbs, and the roses. In 1769, Portolá and his party looked in wonder at the tallest trees they had ever seen. These new trees they had found were redwoods. Father Crespi, who loved plants, wrote, "This new tree has a different color and odor. It is not like anything we have in Spain!" There was plenty of water nearby too. Everyone agreed that this would be a perfect place for a mission.

Seventeen years later Father Lasuén crossed the mountains and came to the same place. He, too, thought it would be a good place for another mission. When he founded the mission, many Indians came to hear him. They stayed to help the padres cut redwood for the buildings. A field was chosen for growing wheat. Gifts from the older missions poured in. Everything seemed to be going well.

The first rainy season they found the church was too near the river. The church

84

Today's church looks as Mission Santa Cruz once did

was rebuilt on higher land. This church was a strong adobe one with a tower on it. This was the mission of the "Holy Cross" (Santa Cruz).

The crops of wheat did well. Almost every day flour mills were busy grinding wheat. Cooking was done on the adobe stoves and baking in the adobe ovens. These ovens (*hornos*) were round like a beehive. A fire heated the oven until only coals were left. Bread to be baked was put into the oven through an opening in the front. This was then covered with a wooden door. The hot bread was taken out by means of a long paddle. The women liked to bake. The men liked to grow the golden wheat.

The mission seemed to have everything to make it do well. Soon, however, trouble started and it never seemed to end. Word came that the warlike Indians had planned a raid on the mission. Even the Indian neophytes in the mission made trouble. They were restless and said, "We do not want to work. We would rather hunt quail and deer. We would rather fish." There were fewer Indians living at this mission than at any other one. The forests around were full of wild animals, mostly bears. They, too, made trouble. One day a storm came in from the sea. The lands were covered with a flood. The water even came up to the church. Damage was done, but the padres still had courage to go on.

Many years before Father Serra had said, "No mission should be near a pueblo." What he said proved right. There should be lots of land around the missions. Room was needed for growing crops and raising cattle. The mission was like a small city in itself. The people of the pueblo were not like those who lived at the mission. They cared for pleasure more than church.

"The mission Indians are slowly leaving or dying," the people of the pueblo said. "They cannot take care of the land, anyway. Why shouldn't we have it?"

Father Palou said firmly, "A league [about three miles] on all sides of the mission belongs to the Indians. It shall be theirs!"

86

Then the Mexican Government took charge of the Church and the lands. Most of the Indians went back to the hills. Some of the cattle were given away and some went back to the wilds. The Mission of the Holy Cross came to an end. Water came in from the sea again. At last there were only ruins. For fifty years the mission was only a memory.

At last even the ruins were cleared away. Nearby stands another church which looks as Mission Santa Cruz did. It is only half the size of the first church. It shows what the church looked like in the early days. The old robes are still used at Christmas night services. These are the only memories left of the mission that began so well.

Founded
October 9, 1791

MISSION SOLEDAD *where a padre starved*

PORTOLÁ AND FATHER CRESPI were the first white men who had come to the valley between the Salinas River and the Santa Lucia Mountains. As they had made camp for the night, a curious Indian came close by. They tried to talk to him, but he said only one word. It sounded like *"soledad,"* the Spanish word for loneliness. Portolá and Crespi looked over the barren valley. There were no trees growing in the chocolate-brown land. They decided Soledad would be a good name for this lonely place.

Father Lasuén had been told about Soledad. A mission was needed between San Antonio and Carmel. If a mission was founded between the two, it would be a good stopping place on the long road. Soledad was about a day's journey from either mission. Soledad was chosen the place for the thirteenth mission.

Soledad was never a large or happy mission. There was much sickness there. Many Indians died, and others went back to the mountains. Sometimes there was little rain and food was scarce. Father Ibáñez, the padre of Mission Soledad, did not mind. He helped the Indians when they were sick. He kept on in spite of everything. He taught the Indians to read music and to write. He even wrote a Christmas play for them which they gave year after year. They acted out the Christmas story of the shepherds and the angels and the three wise kings.

When Bouchard, the pirate, came to Mission San Carlos at Carmel, people left there quickly. They had to save themselves and the belongings of the mission. They went inland to nearby Mission Soledad. They knew that Father Ibáñez would share the few blankets and little food that he had there.

Father Ibáñez was old, and life was not easy. In summer the adobe rooms were very hot. In winter they were cold and damp. Father Ibáñez found it hard to tend to all his duties. The Indians wanted to help him. They took him to their hot springs in the mountains to make him better. The treatments did not help much. Father Ibáñez's fifteen years at Mission Soledad came to an end.

No one seemed to care much for Mission Soledad. Indians left the mission. No padre wanted to live in this lonely place. Then Father Sarría came to Mission Soledad. He knew that his life there would not be easy but he did not mind. He wanted to spend his last years there and make the mission live again. When a flood washed out the church, a few Indians helped him build another one. It was not a big church. He loved the Indians and gave them all the food he could spare. He did not eat much himself. He became weak with hunger. One day at a service in the church, he fell to the floor. The Indians carried his body through the mountains to Mission San Antonio.

No one came to live at Mission Soledad after that. The rains beat upon the walls and melted away the adobe bricks. Before long only ruins were left. Today the mission church has been rebuilt in the once lonely valley.

90

Founded
June 11, 1797

MISSION SAN JOSÉ *and its Indian orchestra*

THE NEXT MISSION founded was Mission San José. Father Lasuén, president of the missions, wanted to find good places for inland missions. The eastern shore of San Francisco Bay had never been explored! Father Lasuén was now an old man, but he started out on the trip. He had been at Santa Clara for many years. He knew all the land around the bay well. He found a beautiful hillside with a view of the bay. It was here that he founded Mission San José.

The first buildings were made of wood with grass roofs. Later they were made of adobe and red bricks. The brick earth which they found nearby was just right for making bricks and tiles. Not many Indians came to the new mission for a long time. When no Indians came, there were no builders. Building of the mission was very slow, but finally a mission church was built. It was a long one and very plain. The orchard of fruit and olive trees was walled in. A visitor to San José wrote, "There are lots of grapes here. The soil is rich. Even the pigeons have plenty to

92

The padres' rooms are all that remain of Mission San José

eat. This mission should be the richest and best in California!"

Mission San José did not become the richest, but it did become famous for its orchestra. Father Durán was the padre who taught the Indians to make simple flutes, violins, and drums. They had a few music books. Father Durán played and the Indians listened. Then they played what they heard. They played for all the dances, the fiestas, and many of the weddings. The Indians who did not live at Mission San José came for miles to hear them play. On feast days visitors came from Mission Santa Clara and Mission San Francisco. As the visitors came near, the mission bells rang out a welcome. In the mission square, or patio, was the Indian orchestra. The other Indians stood by, beating time with their feet. Dancing Indians in bright feathers seemed to be everywhere. A bear and bull fight usually followed. Again at sunset the bells rang and the guns were fired.

Father Durán lived at the mission for twenty-seven years. He was one of the finest padres of mission days. For many years he taught the Indians to make many things in the shops. He never left San José Mission except to go to Santa Clara on feast days once in a while. In spite of all of his hard work, there was trouble with the Indians.

Finally Mexico took over the missions. Pio Pico, governor of California, sold the mission to his brother. Father Durán was brokenhearted about his Indian orchestra. "It cost me twelve years of work to teach them," he said sadly. He left Mission San José and went to live at Mission Santa Barbara.

After Father Durán left, there were still many good years. There were thousands of head of cattle on the mission lands. There were six thousand grapevines loaded with wine grapes. Then came the gold-rush days in California. Almost overnight the mission became an important place. It was turned into a trading post. Here miners came with their gold to trade it for things to eat and wear. They called it "Mission Saint Joe." Potatoes grown near the old mission were sold to the miners for a very high price. After the gold-rush days the mission was returned to the Franciscans. A short time later there was an earthquake and the walls of the church crumbled into ruins. Nearly all of the other mission buildings fell too. Only the rooms of the padres were left.

In these dark, gloomy rooms can be seen the hand-cut beams and willow branches used in making the roof. They are fastened with strips of leather. Down the slope is a garden with gray-green olive trees. There were more olive trees at this mission than at any other. The trees still bear fruit. These trees and the padres' rooms are the only things that are left to tell us of the Mission San José that was so famous for its Indian music.

MISSION SAN JUAN BAUTISTA
and what its barrel organ did

ONLY TWO WEEKS after Mission San José was founded, Father Lasuén founded Mission San Juan Bautista. A new mission was needed between Mission San Carlos and Mission Santa Clara.

San Juan Bautista started off very well. It was in a valley where there were many Indians, and the first small chapel could not hold all who came. A large church was built for them, a wider church than any other mission had. By the time the church was finished, half of the Indians had gone. The padre closed the arches on each side. Then the church was long and narrow like all the other missions. San Juan Bautista was proud of its bells. There were nine of them, and when they were rung together, they made a beautiful chime.

Father Tapis, a padre at the mission, was interested in music. He picked out the best voices and had a fine Indian boys' choir. He wrote the music notes in black,

San Juan Bautista today

yellow, green, and red. Each boy could follow his part by the color of the notes. It made the Indian boys happy to sing together. They even sang when they worked. Music seemed to make the work easier to do.

Many of the Indians who lived at the mission were Tulare Indians. There were other Tulare Indians who did not come to live at the mission. They caused trouble from time to time. Once they killed some mission Indians and drove away the horses. These mission Indians raced after their horses and brought them back. Suddenly there was a great clatter of horses' hoofs. The warlike Tulares were racing toward the mission! Every mission Indian knew the danger. "The Tulares! The Tulares!" they cried. "Run for your lives!" shouted the men. "Protect our people and our mission," prayed Padre Tapis.

Then the padre thought of something that would help. As the Tulares came near he brought out a barrel organ. Captain Vancouver, an English visitor, had once given it to Mission San Carlos. Now it was at Mission San Juan Bautista. As the handle of the organ was turned, strange music came out of it. The mission Indians did not know the words, but they sang anyway! The Tulares liked the strange music. They wanted to stay at the mission they had come to destroy.

After word came that Mexico owned California, the real mission days were over. The orchards were sold. The mission Indians were free to leave. They were given shares of land and a little money. They were told to care for themselves. It was not long until they went back to the Tulare country. Bandits raided the mission, but there were always some kind padres there. During the gold-rush days the stagecoaches changed horses in the little village by the mission. In those days the pueblo was on the main highway.

The visitor to Mission San Juan Bautista has to turn off the main road a short way to find it. The road leads to the sleepy little village of San Juan Bautista. The plaza in front of the mission was once a place for gay fiestas. Californians loved nothing

Padres spent many hours keeping records of the missions

better than a party or fiesta. Often fiestas were held on special feast days. Then the fiesta began with a service in the church. This church had a long porch or corridor down which the people walked on feast days. First came the chanting padres, then the choir boys, and the mission Indians last. The first and twelfth arches are square. Through these arches they entered and left. After the service there was feasting in the plaza. In the afternoon everyone was ready for games and sports. In the evening there were always music and dancing. The dancing usually lasted until the sun came up next morning.

In the church you can see the old tile floor that has been there all these years. "Look sharply," says the guide. "You can still see the prints of oak leaves in the tiles. The prints of bear and coyote feet are there too. They walked on the bricks when they were drying in the sun."

In the museum you can see the barrel organ that charmed the Tulare Indians. The music copied by Father Tapis is there for you to see too. The famous bells that could be heard eight miles across the valley are gone. The only one left was rung on Sundays and feast days. The quiet garden overlooks the fields and orchard and the little river. It was in these fields that the Indian men worked.

You can see a dusty piece of El Camino Real behind this mission. It is really the path the padres used! It led to Mission San Carlos. In the beginning, El Camino Real, the King's Highway, was probably only a deer trail. Next, perhaps an Indian followed the same path. Then came Portolá and his men. Then a padre traveling from mission to mission. Still later the creaking oxcarts, or *carretas,* came along the road. After that rattling old stagecoaches bumped over the road. Later came the automobile and railroad. Today only a piece of El Camino Real is left there to show us where the padres walked.

MISSION SAN MIGUEL *where Indians painted*

Mission San Miguel, founded by Father Lasuen, was between Mission San Luis Obispo and San Antonio de Padua. Now the northern half of the mission chain was complete. When other missions heard about its founding, most of them sent gifts. The gifts seemed to come from everywhere. Even starving Mission Soledad sent two oxen.

Building went much faster than in the earlier days. More was known about making bricks and tiles by this time. Indians in great numbers came to help. The porch, or corridor, of the mission had sixteen arches because it was the sixteenth mission. No bell tower was built. The bell was hung on a wooden log. In two years all the building was finished, but there were no paintings in the church. Some of the padres were artists, but they had many things to do. They had little time for art. Help was needed in the painting inside the church. The mission fathers sent to Monterey and asked Esteban Munras to come and help. He used red rock dust for

101

the red color and blue from the flowers. He taught the Indians to make the church as beautiful as they could.

This place had seemed a good spot for a mission. There were many Indians nearby. There was water there. Pine trees in the hills could be used for building. There was a place where one could have mud baths. The Indians and the padres enjoyed that! Limestone and clay for bricks were not far from the mission. Later it was found that the soil was poor. The summers were very hot. There was not enough rain. All this meant that the crops were poor. The mission was not so lucky as the others because of that.

The time came when Mexico took charge of the missions. For a while there was a guard at Mission San Miguel but no padres. The mission was without land or cattle, and the Indians were gone. Governor Pico sent word to the Indians to come back or the land would be sold. They did not come back.

William Reid bought the mission. He lived there with his Spanish wife and family. He had a store in part of it. One night he had some soldiers in for a party. He told them that he had lots of sheep and lots of money. They left, but they came back again. In the room that is now a museum, Mr. Reid and his whole family were murdered! The soldiers who killed them left with the gold and other things of value.

No one lived in the mission for many years after that. Every evening at sundown an old Indian neophyte came back and rang the bell. Mission San Miguel was on the main road between San Francisco and Los Angeles. During the gold-rush days the gold seekers stopped by the old mission and spent the night.

Then the padres came again and planted flowers in the garden and built the walls. Today the visitor will find this mission on the highway just as it used to be. The very large bell which hangs on a wooden log is rung three times a day. In the padre's kitchen the round oven still stands. An old wine vat is there. In the

Indians built strong thick adobe walls brick by brick

mission are tools used in those days. There are a spinning wheel and loom, fish traps and branding irons. There is a "mission window" made of cowhide, shaved and greased. These windows were used in cold or wet weather. There is a wishing chair which has a story. One of the padres said to an Indian girl:

"Concha, sit in the chair and make a wish." She sat in the chair and made a wish. A week later she had a husband!

Once more the mission is a friendly place. For fifty years the Franciscans have worn brown robes instead of gray. Today the brown-robed padres show the visitors with pride the red-and-blue painting in the church. Many years have passed since the Indians and Esteban Munras made them. People still like to look at the painting and think of the time when Indians and padres worked there together.

San Miguel today is a friendly place

*Founded
September 8, 1797*

MISSION SAN FERNANDO *where travelers found a welcome*

AN EXPLORING PARTY was sent from Mission San Buenaventura to find a good place for another mission. It was to be between that mission and Mission San Gabriel. The party came back and told about a wide valley called Encino (Oaks). It was here that they decided to have the seventeenth mission, Mission San Fernando. It was not far away from the pueblo, Los Angeles.

Mission San Fernando was one of the largest missions. There were so many Indians that the buildings had to be made bigger and bigger. The long building was the padres' house, and it took a long time to build. It was one of the longest of any of the missions and had nineteen arches.

This mission became famous for its ironwork. The Indians made plows, tools, cattle brands, hinges, and scissors. They traded them to other missions and to ships.

There were many acres of fine grapevines. When the grapes ripened, it was time for wine making. Juice was pressed from grapes by barefoot Indians. First

106

The padres' house at Mission San Fernando

they washed their feet in a little basin. They climbed low ladders into the wine vats. The red juice drained into wooden pipes and then into barrels in a room below. The juice was left in a cool room until it turned to wine. The wine was sold to the pueblos and the presidios.

The mission was just like a well-run little city. The sunrise bell called the Indians to church and then to a simple breakfast of *atole,* or corn mush. An Indian took a wooden bowl and went to the patio, or square. Here women were cooking *atole* in large kettles. A woman put enough *atole* in the bowl for the whole family. It was then taken hurriedly back to the little Indian hut. The young unmarried men and women took their food from a big kettle in the mission patio. After breakfast there was work for everyone to do. While the men and boys were busy in the fields and with the building, the women spun long threads of wool. The older children had some time for study with the padres. Sometimes they were kept busy running errands or shooing the birds from the fruit trees in the orchards. Noon was the rest period. The meal at noon was *atole* with meat and vegetables added. Sometimes there were *tortillas,* or flat cakes of ground meal. Everyone rested for two hours and then went to work again. The bells called them to church again later, and then came supper. The supper was about the same as breakfast. Sometimes there was fruit. The evening was the time for singing and dancing until it was time to go to bed.

Mission San Fernando was a stopping place for many travelers. An Indian stood at the door ready to unsaddle the horses. A stranger knew he would be welcome here or at any other mission. The padres had to be innkeepers as well as farmers and builders and teachers. They liked to have visitors stop for the night. In this way the padres could hear news from other places. The rawhide beds were not very comfortable, but strangers were glad to stay. The *sala,* or dining room, was the largest in any of the missions. A dining table was used that was let down from the ceiling at mealtime. The kitchen had a clay-and-rock stove along the back wall. On it was cooked all the meals for the padres and the visitors. When the visitor was ready to leave, the padre gave him a lunch and a horse to use. There was nothing to pay. As time went on, strangers stopped at the mission almost every day, and all found a welcome.

One year there were many rats at Mission San Fernando. They seemed to eat everything in sight. The padres sent to their friends at Mission San Gabriel and asked them what to do. They knew that they, too, had had rats in their storerooms. Two cats were sent to Mission San Fernando to catch rats.

"But how will the cats get in and out of the mission?" asked one of the Indians.

"Why, we can cut holes in the corners of the mission doors!" a padre answered.

Holes were cut in the corners of the heavy mission doors. The cats could go in and out as they pleased.

Many years passed. The missions came under the control of Mexico. For a time the mission was rented and then sold. It was used as a storeroom and a stable. Rats ate the robes and linens. Many things of value were taken away from the church. The winter rains washed down the walls.

About this time an exciting thing happened near the mission. A rancher on the mission lands pulled up a bunch of wild onions. He found that the soil around the roots had some shiny, yellow dust! He dug again and found some more! It turned out to be real gold. He ran to tell his friends. The gold dust was sent to a city in the East to be made into gold coins. The first "gold pans" were Indian baskets in the shapes of shallow bowls. The mission did not get anything from the discovery of gold. Oil was found near the mission too. In Pico Canyon a man was watching his sheep. He saw thick, black oil coming out of the ground. He took some to the mission. No one seemed to find any interest in it. Fifteen years later the first oil well in California was drilled in this same canyon.

Mission San Fernando has all been rebuilt. One wall of the old church is leaning to one side. It is just as the Indians made it. The long padres' house with the arches is in front. Inside one cannot miss seeing the holes in the doors for the cats. There are the rooms where wine was made and kept. Across the street is a park called Memory Garden. Plants from other missions have been brought there. A statue of Father Serra is near a large star-shaped fountain. Here Indian children used to play. Those who see the gardens and the mission think of other days. They are reminded of the time when all Indians and travelers were welcome there.

Founded
June 13, 1798

MISSION SAN LUIS REY *the richest mission*

MISSION SAN LUIS REY was the last mission to be founded by Father Lasuén. He had started five missions in one year. Many visitors came to see the founding of the eighteenth mission. They wanted to see the rich valley in which this mission would be built. Father Lasuén watched the Indians put up two rooms made of poles and branches of trees. He told them where to put the padres' house and the church. He stayed and taught them how to plant grain. Then he went on his way north and left Father Peyri to see that all went well.

Everything did go well from the very start. The Indians were glad to come to the new mission. Father Peyri worked side by side with them. He was a great builder and planned everything well. Some of the Indians went to faraway Mount Palomar and brought back logs for the church. The church was built in the shape of a large cross. The only other one built like that was at Mission San Juan Capistrano.

111

The "King of the Missions," as it was called, was all done in ten years. It was the largest of all the missions built by the padres. It had more than two hundred arches. A visitor said, "From a distance it looks like a white palace!" Mission San Luis Rey had more Indians than the others. It became one of the richest of all the missions. There were miles and miles of golden waves of ripe wheat. Some of it was sent to Mexico and Spain. The storerooms of the mission were full. There were huge gardens of vegetables of all kinds. The vines were heavy with sweet purple grapes. Mission San Luis Rey had lots of fine wine. Only the missions in the south made wine because the grapes grew best in warm weather. San Luis Rey had the most and the best.

There were many thousands of cattle on the mission lands. After the cattle were killed, a big fire was built under large iron kettles. These kettles came from whaling ships. Into the kettles the Indians threw the fat parts. Soon the kettles were full of clear boiling grease. When the fat, or tallow, was cold it was hard and solid. Part of the tallow was made into soap. Hundreds of gallons of soap were boiled at one time. Some of the tallow was made into candles. A candlemaker hung short pieces of string on a wheel. As he turned the wheel slowly, he poured the melted tallow down the string. As the tallow cooled, more tallow was poured. With each turn of the wheel the candles grew larger. These candles helped to light the small dark adobe rooms and the mission church.

Father Peyri loved his Indian friends. When the Mexican Government told the padres to leave the missions he did not want to say good-by. He was getting old and he decided to go back to Spain. He slipped away by night and went to San Diego. When his friends heard about it, they got on their horses. They rode to San Diego to bring him back. They got there just as he was leaving. Two of his Indian friends were on the boat with him. Some tried to swim to the boat. When the Indians went back to the mission, they missed him very much. They put candles and flowers

in front of his picture. They prayed for his return, but he never came back.

San Luis Rey was a rich mission, and Governor Pico decided to take it for himself. When he went back to Mexico, the mission was left all alone. A woman who lived on a rancho nearby took some of the paintings and bells to her home to care for them. She thought that someday the mission would want them back again. Wood and tiles were taken away for houses and barns. Much of the roof fell. The dome fell also. Weeds grew up between the tiles on the floor. For nearly fifty years the mission was left to the wind and the rain. Only visitors came to see the broken building.

Many years later two Franciscans were looking for a place to have a school. They wanted a place for young men to study. Mission San Luis Rey looked like a good place. A school was started and is still there today. The walls were put up again. The old fountains were uncovered. The bells rang from the tower again. The old treasures were brought back. A service was held when the buildings were done. Many people came to see it again. Once more San Luis Rey was "King of the Missions."

Those who go to see Mission San Luis Rey now will find much to interest them. In the church may be seen bright paintings in Indian design. There are many robes with bright gold and silver threads. Some that were brought from Spain are more than three hundred years old. There is a wide padre's hat that was worn in the hot sun. There is a padre's walking stick. On it is a hook. On the hook he carried his prayer book and food in a little bundle when he went on a journey. Much new building has been done. Now the mission looks much as it did when Father Peyri planned and left it many years ago.

Mission San Luis Rey — king of the missions

Founded
September 17, 1804

MISSION SANTA INÉS *and the Indian saddle makers*

AMONG THE OAKS in the valley of what is now Santa Barbara County, the Chumash Indians lived. The Chumash Indians knew how to make blankets out of feathers. Their baskets were brightly colored. They went to the mountain slopes and got wood for their long canoes. They made paintings of animals on cliffs or in caves. They loved a waterfall named Nojoqui. It gave them water when other streams went dry. Some of the Indians lived at Mission Santa Barbara. Others lived at Mission La Purísima. There were many Chumash Indians who lived far from either mission. Father Tapis, the new president of the missions, wanted to found a mission for them. Besides, Mission Santa Barbara and Mission La Purísima were a long distance apart. With the new mission, each mission would be about a day's journey apart. This is the way the chain of missions had been planned.

With some soldiers Father Tapis set out over the mountains behind Santa

116

Mission Santa Inés has changed very little

Barbara. He went down into the valleys and past Nojoqui Falls. From the falls he came to a river. He decided that Mission Santa Inés would be there.

Mission Santa Inés grew fast. Even the earthquake of 1812 did not stop the building. A large rock basin was built in front of the mission. Here the hides that were made into saddles were soaked and stretched. After the saddles were made, the leather was carved into designs. Often they were works of art. The silverworkers made beautiful silver designs too. The missions and ranchos admired the saddles and wanted them for their fine horses. Californians were always proud of their horses and saddles. Some of the old Santa Inés saddles may still be found in California.

While all was peaceful at the mission, the Tulare Indians inland were planning an attack on the missions. They liked the padres, but some of the Indians had trouble with the soldiers. Living among the Tulares was an Indian girl named Pasquala. She had lived at the mission until the Tulares had carried her away. She was afraid when she heard the Tulares planning to attack the mission. She knew there was only one thing for her to do. It was to get to the mission to warn the padres before the Tulares came. Through the rocky hills and valleys Pasquala ran as fast as she could. When she reached the mission, she shouted to Padre Uria, "Padre! War! War!" Padre Uria and the soldiers made ready for the attack. With some soldiers from Santa Barbara they fought off the Tulares. No one at the mission was killed, but Pasquala was not so lucky. The Indian girl who saved Mission Santa Inés died from running too hard. Padre Uria was very sorry. He decided to bury her in the church, even though Indians were usually buried outside.

After Mexico won California from the Spanish, there were no Indians left at the mission. Father Buckler came to Santa Inés to stay a few weeks. He stayed for twenty years. Weasels, snakes, and rats lived in rooms with leaky roofs. Father Buckler dug and swept and plastered. He welcomed all travelers on the road. He gave them supper and invited them to stay for the night. They did, and they often

118

stayed for a long time to help him fix up parts of the mission.

Today a padre will let you see the mission. Old robes and music books are in the museum. You can see the high windows that were built to protect the church from the warlike Tulares. You can see the arches painted red. Little seems to have changed since Father Tapis founded this mission for the Chumash Indians.

*Founded
December 14, 1817*

MISSION SAN RAFAEL *and how the Indians were cured*

NINETEEN MISSIONS had now been founded. The chain of missions from San Diego to San Francisco seemed complete. But two more missions in the north were to be added to the chain. One was Mission San Rafael, which was founded because of the sickness of the Indians of Mission San Francisco.

Many Indians of Mission San Francisco had come from warm sunny valleys and were not used to the fogs and winds of San Francisco. Many of them became sick. The mission fathers decided to take the Indians across the bay to a sunny valley they knew. At first there was no real mission there. San Rafael was only a small group of Indians cared for by a padre. The padre had been a doctor and knew how to cure the sick Indians.

About this time another padre came to a mission just north of San Rafael at Sonoma. He tried to close San Rafael. He wanted all the Indians from San Rafael and Mission San Francisco to come to his mission. San Rafael was not closed. It was made a real mission instead.

The new Mission San Rafael resembles the old one

All was not well at Mission San Rafael. There was a strong Indian chief nearby called Marin. He made trouble for the mission guard. The padre asked the Spanish soldiers to help them. Marin lost in the battle. His name is well remembered in the name of Marin County which surrounds the town of San Rafael today.

Mission San Rafael was never very large or very well built. After the mission was sold, no one seemed to care about it. The padres and the Indians were gone. Sometimes the people nearby would come there for parties or dances. As the town of San Rafael grew up around the mission, the mission was forgotten. The tiles and bells disappeared. The walls crumbled away. Only a pear tree was left where a fine orchard once stood.

Now a new mission building which looks like the old one has been built near the spot where the old one stood. There is little else to remind us of the mission where sick Indians of San Francisco were made well.

MISSION SAN FRANCISCO DE SOLANO
the mission farthest north

FATHER ALTIMIRA founded this last mission. When he was sent from Spain to Mission San Francisco, twenty of the twenty-one missions had been founded. Many of them were not so rich as they once had been. Father Altimira did not think, however, that the missions were going to end so soon. He thought that Spain should have another mission even farther north than San Rafael.

One day, with some soldiers from San Francisco, Father Altimira set out. He explored the valleys north of San Rafael and found a good spot. The Indians called it Sonoma, or "Valley of the Moon." He did not ask the president of the missions if another mission could be founded. He said it was needed to keep the Russians from coming south and he would found it himself. He named it Mission San Francisco de Solano.

After Father Altimira had founded this new mission, he went to Monterey. He

123

wanted to interest the governor of California in his plan. He wanted to build a great new mission in Sonoma. He wanted the padres to give up Mission San Rafael and Mission San Francisco. He thought that this new mission should be the only one in northern California. The governor agreed to his plans. The mission fathers heard about it and they did not agree. Finally, however, they let Father Altimira go on with the new mission. They did not give up Mission San Rafael and Mission San Francisco. Warlike Indians did not like Father Altimira's mission. They drove him away from the mission. Later he went back to Spain.

When Mexico took California from Spain, a famous Mexican general, Mariano Vallejo, stayed at Mission San Francisco de Solano. He defeated the Indians, but he could not defeat the Americans. Every day more Americans came to California. The Americans took General Vallejo prisoner and raised the famous Bear Flag near the mission. California was no longer ruled by Mexico. Soon it was to become a part of the United States.

Today the mission has been rebuilt. It is now a California state park. It is used as a museum. In it are old pictures and other things which tell about early California. Mission San Francisco de Solano is just a small, plain building. It reminds us of the missions that stretched up to it all the way from San Diego. It reminds us of all the missions and the Indians and padres whose work makes this story.

Mission San Francisco de Solano tells the story of early mission days

HOW TO PRONOUNCE SPANISH NAMES AND WORDS

adobe,   ah do' bay
Alameda,   Ah lah may' dah
Altimira,   Al tee mee' ra
atole,   ah toh' lay
Anza,   Ahn' sah
Bouchard,   Boo shard'
carreta,   kah ray' tah
Cabrillo,   Kah bree' o
Catalá, F.,   Cat a lah'
Crespi, F.,   Kres' pee
de la Cuesta, F.,   de la Coo es' tah
Dolores, Mission,   Do lo' rays
Durán, E.,   Doo' rahn
El Camino Real,   Ayl Kah mee'noh Ray ahl'
Encino,   En see' noh
fiesta,   fee ace' tah
Galvez,   Gahl' vays
Gaspar de Portolá,   Gahs pahr' day Pohr toh lah'
Ibáñez, F.,   E bahn' yes
Jayme, F.,   Hi' may
Junípero,   Hoo nee' pare oh
La Paz,   La Pahs'
Lasuén,   Lah soo en'
Martinez, F.,   Mar tee' nes
metate,   may tah' tay
Monterey,   Mohn tay ray'
Munras, Esteban,   Moon' ras Es tay' bahn
neophyte,   nee' oh fite
Nojoqui,   No ho' kee
padre,   pah' dray
palomino,   pal o mee' noh
Palou, F.,   Pah low'
Pasquala,   Pahs cooah' lah
Payeras, F.,   Pa yher' ahs

Peyri, F.,   Pay' ree
Pico, Pio,   Pee' koh Pee' oh
presidio,   pray see' dee oh
pueblo,   poo ay' blow
Rivera,   Ree vay' rah
San Antonio,   Sahn Ahn tohn' ee oh
San Buenaventura,   Sahn Boo ay nah ven too' rah
San Carlos,   Sahn Cahr' lohs
San Diego,   Sahn Dee ay' go
San Fernando,   Sahn Fer nahn' do
San Francisco Solano,   Sahn Frahn cees' co So lah' no
San Gabriel,   Sahn Gah bree el'
San José,   Sahn Ho say'
San Juan Bautista,   Sahn Whan Bow tees' tah
San Juan Capistrano,   Sahn Whan Cah pees trah' no
San Luis Obispo,   Sahn Loo' ees Oh bees' po
San Luis Rey,   Sahn Loo' ees Ray'
San Miguel,   Sahn Mee gell'
San Rafael,   Sahn Rah fay ell'
Santa Barbara,   Sahn' tah Bahr' bahr ah
Santa Clara,   Sahn' tah Clah' rah
Santa Cruz,   Sahn' tah Croos
Santa Inés,   Sahn' tah Ee nays'
Sarría, F.,   Sah ree' ah
Serra,   Sare' ah
Soledad,   So' leh dahd
Tapis, F.,   Tah' pees
tortilla,   tohr tee' ya
Tulares,   Too lahr' ace
tule,   too' lay
Vancouver,   Van coo' vehr
Viceroy,   Vees' a roy
Vizcaíno,   Vees kah ee' no